Stories
for YOU

"A Wish for You" A First Grader's Story from 1957

RICKY KENNISON

AuthorHouse™
1663 Liberty Drive
Bloomington, IN 47403
www.authorhouse.com
Phone: 1 (800) 839-8640

Published by AuthorHouse 06/22/2016

ISBN: 978-1-5246-1461-4 (sc)
ISBN: 978-1-5246-1462-1 (e)

Library of Congress Control Number: 2016909908

Print information available on the last page.

Any people depicted in stock imagery provided by Thinkstock are models, and such images are being used for illustrative purposes only. Certain stock imagery © Thinkstock.

This book is printed on acid-free paper.

Because of the dynamic nature of the Internet, any web addresses or links contained in this book may have changed since publication and may no longer be valid. The views expressed in this work are solely those of the author and do not necessarily reflect the views of the publisher, and the publisher hereby disclaims any responsibility for them.

authorHOUSE®

This book is dedicated to my deceased wife.

Contents

"A WISH FOR YOU"
A first graders story from 1957

A trip to my first year in school- first grade. The year was 1957at North Kansas City, Missouri elementary school. There was no lunch room. A lunch cart pushed by a server stopped at each room with plates and hot food on the cart. At the classroom door we would form lines from rows of desks where we sat . The server would take a plate, and put the food on the plate for us to eat. There were no choices of what to take from the cart. We got what ever was on the pushcart.

Early in the morning we would line up by the sink in the back of the classroom from rows at our desks. Mrs. Earlee would give each of us a vitamin tablet and a paper cup of water at the sink. We would return to our seats at our desks. There was no breakfast served at all just vitamins and lunch.

Mrs. Earlee would have us do projects. One day she told us about the weather (partly cloddy or partly sunny). We would each take turns in the morning going to the classroom window, and looking out reporting to the class partly cloddy or partly sunny or just sunny.

My room was right inside the entrance doors to the school, then turn left. I was in the first room. The school was on one level- no upstairs or downstairs. Next to the school was a public park. Down the street from the school was a public library. The school had no library . Mrs. Earlee would take us to the public library to get books. We would form a single line inside of the class room and follow the one in front of us . She would walk us outside of the school single file. The public library was down the street about four blocks. Inside the library we would look for books to take with us to read. After selecting a book to read, Mrs. Earlee would walk us back down the sidewalk on the street to the school and our classroom.

Mrs. Earlee one day decided to take us to the public park next to the school. We lined up like we did for the library. We walked and walked to the public park next to the school. She gathered us all around her. Mrs. Earlee told us she was going to have a contest with a prize for the winner. Its been along time since 1957.

I can not remember the prize she had for us but I remember we were all excited to win. Mrs. Earlee had a box of saltine crackers and she said, " the contest goes like this." Everyone was to eat one cracker when she said go. The first student who could whistle would win the prize. We were all excited and jumping and moving around to get a saltine cracker.

One girl said to me she couldn't whistle and she asked me to whistle for her. My reaction was to tell her I was going to whistle for myself. The little girl asked the little boy standing next to us if he would whistle for her because she couldn't whistle. I didn't hear the little boy's answer.

Mrs. Earlee told us all to get ready to eat the cracker then she said go. We all put the crackers in our mouths and began chewing.

Some how the little girl who couldn't whistle finished first. She asked me to whistle for her. I tried to whistle but my mouth was too dry from eating the cracker. The little girl seen I couldn't whistle. She asked the little boy she had asked earlier to whistle for her.

He whistled. Mrs. Earlee was excited. Mrs. Earlee said he was the winner. The little boy told Mrs. Earlee the little girl had finished first, but couldn't whistle. He was whistling for her. What a surprise for all of us!

I have always wished it was me who whistled for the little girl even though I couldn't whistle at that time.

My wish as a grew older was to always be like the boy who whistled for the little girl, when she couldn't for herself.

A wish for you is to be the one who whistles for the little girl who can't. The End.

"Grandmother Emma's "Secret Recipe"
Loving and Caring, a first graders story from 1957

Grandmother's secret recipe - oh so good. Grandmother always gave a lot of loving and caring. She always made me feel special. Grandmother lived with Grandfather in a little house next to the Missouri River.

There was a man made levee between her house and the river. A man use to cut the grass on the levee on her side of the levee with horses. The horses pulled the rolling knives that cut the grass. I was small and I use to like to watch the horses pull the blades that rolled and cut the grass.

There were bridges on both sides of grandmother's house that crossed the Missouri river. On the top side of the bridges cars crossed and on the underside of the bridge trains crossed the river. My uncle Everett, my grandmother's oldest son, would take me across the levee to fish in the river. We sometimes caught fish and it was a lot of fun.

In the back yard at grandmother's house she had a pump for pumping water out of the ground. She had water in the house now, but still used the pump sometimes. The pump was painted red. From time to time homeless men would travel past the back of grandmother's house along the levee between the bridges. Back then these homeless men were called hobos. They rode the rails of the trains from place to place. Many times they would stop by grandmother's house and say they were hungry or thirsty. Grandmother always said she would fix something for them. Usually she had a roll of bologna she would slice herself. Often the sliced bologna was sliced uneven when she made the sandwiches. The slices of bologna usually was cut thick on one edge, and thin on the other edge.

She would tell me to pump some water from the well for the men to drink. The pump still worked. The homeless men were always so thankful to Grandmother. They smiled waving their arm as they walked away towards the bridges. If the homeless men asked for another bologna sandwich grandmother would always give them one. Grandfather said the homeless men would place a mark somewhere for the others to see. The mark was showing where others could get something to eat. I guess Grandfather knew because a lot of homeless men would stop and say they were hungry. Of course grandmother would always give them a bologna sandwich, and a tin glass of water from the pump outside.

Grandmother has been gone for along time now, but her secret recipe - Loving and Caring still lives on..

Try grandmother's secret recipe sometimes. It's a lot of fun! The End.

WASP ON THE CEILING

Mr. Wasp what are doing on the kitchen ceiling? Your are suppose to be outside in your own house. I see you there Mr. Wasp as I lay back in my easy chair by the kitchen table. Seems like you don't know where you are at. Your house I seen by the garage door when I drive the care inside. You must have came in the garage when the garage door opened for the car. Inside the house you came when the door from the garage to the inside of the house opened. Now your looking for you way outside. Your not going to be able to open the door to go out on your own.

I could get some spray and spray you. I could get a fly swatter and smash you or get a paper and smash you. You keep trying to get out. You fly to the large glass window by my chair and crawl all around the glass looking for any way out. I still think I should smash you to the glass with a fly swatter. You can sting me and it hurts.

Your just trying to get out on your own. You keep crawling on the glass from corner to corner looking for a way outside. What if I give you a chance? So maybe I'll help you get out. I'll grab you with two fingers by the back of your wings and open the door and let you go outside. This hurts your wings and maybe you can turn around, and sting me with your tail. So I got an idea Mr. Wasp. I bought some small plastic cups with lids the other day. I'll trap you to the glass with an inverted plastic cup. Slide the lid between you and the glass to seal the plastic cup, thus trapping you inside the plastic cup. I can open the door to the outside and release you to the outside again. You might find your house by the garage. I'll give it a try Mr. Wasp. No promises. Don't sting me with your tail.

It works! Mr. Wasp is set free! To my surprise Mr. Wasp stops as soon as he is back outside. He turns to me and says, " I'll bring you good fortune!"

You never know where your good fortune might come from, so look inside your heart it might be right on the kitchen ceiling.
The End.

"SUK'S MAGIC DRY CLEAN MACHINE

Suk is my wife's name. She owns a dry clean business she recently bought. The dry clean business cleans the clothes by using a dry clean machine much like a big washing machine cleans clothes. The clothes go in dirty when the machine stops the clothes are clean.

The dry clean business is an old business and the dry clean machine is very old. Part of the controls on the dry clean machine don't work. The automatic control for the automatic run cycle doesn't function properly so we can't use that control. This makes us clean the clothes on the manual operation control only. We have to know which buttons to push, and how many minutes they must run before we push the next button. This makes a lot of work for us but that is the only way the machine will operate. There is about twenty buttons to push from start to finish. A lot of buttons to push. You have to know when in the cleaning cycle to push the next button. The whole cleaning process takes about forty-five minutes.

When the old owners were showing us how to operate the buttons on the old dry clean machine, they showed us a green button and told us, "never, never, never push the green button"

Suk asks," what will happen if we push the green button?" The old owner answered, " no one knows." " No one has ever pushed the green button before," but he says again, " never push the green button." Suk says, " okay we won't ever push the green button!"

We found out after we bought the dry cleaners the dry clean business is a tough business to make money. We were having problems paying all the expenses and employees. We found out later lots of the dry clean businesses have this financial situation.

Suk says to me, "think positive look up and pray to God something will happen."

We are running the dry clean business and the dry clean machine for a long while when all of a sudden we accidentally pushed the green button. We were scared. What will we do now? The dry clean machine kept running, and running, and running. We couldn't control it by pushing any of the other buttons. It run for about three hours none stop. All of a sudden things got quiet and the dry clean machine stopped. We looked in the glass door of the dry clean machine. We could see the clothes. The clothes looked okay.

We slowly opened the dry clean door and the clothes still looked okay. We started to take the clothes out of the dry clean machine slowly at first. We carefully checked to see if anything was wrong. All of a sudden we seen money - green paper money. Lots of green paper money. We were scared. What could we do? Where did this money come from? We didn't know any answers. We thought for awhile and we came up with only one answer. It must have been the green button we pushed accidentally. No one had ever pushed that button before.

After that happened, we thanked God and promised to only push the green button for green paper money in emergencies.

A true story about green paper money coming out of and old dry clean machine. What do you think about where the green paper money came from?

Thank You God. We needed the money to keep our dry clean business going.
The End.

ELIZABETH WEARS BABY SOCKS

Early in the morning when Suk and I (Ricky) are getting ready for work at the dry cleaners (a store we own) Elizabeth wants to go. Elizabeth is our dog. Elizabeth goes down the stairs and waits by the garage door. Suk makes sure Elizabeth eats her breakfast and Suk gives Elizabeth seizer medicine. Elizabeth has seizers. The veterinarian prescribes the medicine for Elizabeth. When we are finished getting ready to leave for work in the morning, we go to the garage door and open the door. We go into the garage and turn on the light. We push the garage door button that makes the electric garage door open. Suk goes to the car on the passenger side. She gets in the car ready to leave.

I put on my tennis shoes on by slipping them on my feet, while setting in the plastic chair by the garage door. I get up from the chair, open the garage door, and enter the garage. All this time I am pulling the door to the garage shut behind me. I stop and turn off the house lights by the stairs. Elizabeth starts jumping on the door and trying to push the door back open. I slowly pull the door knob shut. I stop a few times pulling the door shut to tell Elizabeth who is barking at the top of her voice. "You can't go." Elizabeth keeps barking at the top of her voice. I say, " you can't go Elizabeth." She keeps barking and jumping up and down. She is barking and jumping up and down on the bottom stair step.

That is how Elizabeth broke he toe nail on her paw - jumping up and down on the bottom stair step. All Elizabeth's toe nails had grown very long. We forgot to take her to the veterinarian to get her nails cut. Elizabeth jumping up and down on the bottom step must have caused he toe nail to break in half. We Didn't know at the time Elizabeth broke her toe nail. Elizabeth would keep barking all the time when Suk and I left for work at the dry cleaners.

When Suk and I got home one day from work at the dry cleaners, we came in the house late around seven in the evening. There was no Elizabeth to greet us as normal at the garage door when we came into the house.

Suk and I went in the house from the garage calling Elizabeth by her name. She didn't answer us by coming to greet us. We went up about seven steps into the living room and found Elizabeth lying on the sofa. She didn't want to get up. Suk and I kept calling Elizabeth to get up and come to us but Elizabeth wouldn't get up. Suk and I went up seven more steps to the kitchen and Elizabeth finally got up. She was holding one paw up, and barely walking with the other three paws. We called her name again, and Elizabeth wobbled up the stairs to the kitchen on three paws holding one paw up.

I picked up Elizabeth and looked at the paw she had been holding up. I couldn't see anything wrong. I moved her toe nails. One toe nail was broken, but still hanging on. She must have broken her toe nail that morning, while jumping on the bottom step by the garage door.

I called the dog doctor (the veterinarian). The veterinarian said to bring Elizabeth to be examined. We took Elizabeth that afternoon to the doctor. The doctor said Elizabeth would have to stay at the doctor's office over night. The dog doctor was going to put Elizabeth to sleep, and operate on Elizabeth's toe nail. I said, " okay." I left Elizabeth with the doctor.

The next day the doctor called, and said Elizabeth could come home. The doctor had cut the toe nail completely out of Elizabeth's paw. The veterinarian said it would grow back.

When the doctor brought Elizabeth out for Suk and I, there was a bandage on Elizabeth's front paw. The doctor said for Suk and I to change the bandage on Elizabeth's paw in 24 hours. We were to put a baby sock on Elizabeth's paw held on by tape, and have her wear it. The doctor said the sock would keep Elizabeth from licking her foot.

So Elizabeth wore baby socks for about two weeks until her foot healed.

Elizabeth wears baby socks what a dog story!
The End.

Printed in the United States
by Baker & Taylor Publisher Services